31 DAYS
— OF —
WEALTH
EMPOWERMENT
for
Women

Simple Tips to Create
Wealth That Lasts

PATTI FAGAN

31 Days of Wealth Empowerment for Women

Patti Fagan, 1st Edition

ISBN (eBook) 979-8-9906178-0-3
ISBN (paperback) 979-8-9906178-1-0

Book cover image credit 99 Designs
Edited by Heather Mize

A Special Gift for You

Thank you so much for purchasing my book. I am confident that you have what it takes to create wealth that lasts.

That's why I created a special companion guide to help you become a wealth empowered woman who takes charge of her destiny. *The Financial Organizer for Busy Women* is filled with worksheets, trackers, goal-setting pages, monthly pages, and journal prompts to help you on your financial empowerment journey.

You can claim your gift for FREE at
PattiFagan.com/Financially-Savvy-Women

Here's to your wealth empowerment!
Patti Fagan

For women, financial independence is a matter of necessity.

~Carrie Schwab-Pomerantz,
President of Charles Schwab Foundation
and leading advocate for financial literacy

Table of Contents

Introduction

Your Wealth Heiress lies within.
It is up to you to take action and make her a reality.

~Linda P. Jones, Wealth Mentor and author of
*3 Steps to Quantum Wealth: The Wealth Heiress' Guide
to Financial Freedom by Investing in Cryptocurrencies*

The potential to be a wealth-empowered woman exists within you. With the proper resources, education, and support, you can rule your financial destiny and create a life you truly love. That's the good news. The bad news is that women face unique financial challenges that men do not—and it's gotten worse since the pandemic. According to a new study by the Transamerica Center for Retirement Studies, "More than half of working women (51%) say their financial situation has been negatively impacted by the pandemic."[1]

Additionally,

- ❖ Women spend more time out of the workforce through-out their careers caring for children or aging parents, meaning they earn less over their lifetime.

---

[1] https://www.nextavenue.org/future-for-retirement-security-women/

❖ Women still earn less than men.

❖ More women work part-time, preventing them from qualifying to participate in workplace retirement plans.

❖ Women contribute less to Social Security, resulting in lower benefits and less retirement income from Social Security.

❖ Women live longer than men.

However, the biggest financial hurdle women face is longevity. According to experts, women will outlive their male counterparts by an average of six years. According to a Merrill Lynch study, *Women & Financial Wellness: Beyond the Bottom Line (2018)*, "Women need to plan for a 100+ year life."[2]

> *"Longevity is a critical issue for women, probably one of the biggest reasons why women's needs are so different than men's in terms of financial saving and investing."*
>
> ~Annamaria Lusardi Ph.D., Academic Director, Global Financial Literacy Excellence Center

Back to the good news. Despite these challenges, you can get excited about *your* financial future.

---

[2] https://www.investopedia.com/personal-finance/women-should-plan-100-year-life-merrill-lynch

In this book, I'm sharing 31 days of wealth-building nuggets to help motivate you to create wealth that lasts. The more women I talk to, the more I realize how common a lack of financial confidence is. Many of my coaching clients have told me they fear making major financial decisions, such as where to invest their money. So, they do nothing and leave money on the table. I'm constantly amazed at the number of women who tell me the majority of their savings is sitting in cash. The #1 reason they cite is feeling intimidated at the thought of investing and growing their wealth.

If this sounds like you, you're not alone. I know that the thought of investing can be daunting. But that doesn't have to stop you. By taking baby steps to learn how to create lasting wealth, you can create financial security for yourself and your loved ones.

Before we get started, let me properly introduce myself.

I'm Patti Fagan, a Master Solutions Master Financial Coach, former retirement planner, and sought-after speaker on women, money, and retirement. For over sixteen years, I've been helping women take charge of their finances and create financial security. I owned and operated an independent insurance and financial services agency for nine of those years. My focus is **helping women achieve financial security for their retirement years.**

In this book, I share everything I've learned from my sixteen-plus years of working with women from all walks of life as a retirement planner and financial coach. These wealth-producing strategies will enable you to pay off debt, save enough for a secure retirement, take care of yourself, and leave a legacy for your loved ones. The simple, beginner-level wealth creation tips will prepare you to create wealth for yourself.

For instance, by creating wealth, you'll be able to do things like pay for your child's college education, which is what my client Maryann did. She came to me after her divorce. At the time, her son was five, and she had $26,000 in credit card debt. Her main concern was being able to give her son a quality college education. So, we created a debt payoff plan and value-based spending plan, which included monthly contributions to savings for her son's future. After paying off her credit cards, she saved enough to invest in a rental property. By the time her son graduated high school, she had saved enough to put him through college. Now, her rental property is helping her fund her retirement. Imagine what it would feel like to not only be able to do things for your loved ones but create a life you love and fund your retirement, too. Well, you can when you prioritize creating wealth.

I know what it's like to be financially disempowered and have nothing to your name. Although I'm a money coach now, there was a time when I was clueless about money. I was a classic financial avoider. Not taking wealth building seriously got me into trouble with six-figure credit card debt from a failed partnership almost twenty years ago. Thankfully, after a lot of deep inner money work, I was able to pay it all off in approximately five years without having to file for bankruptcy. The key to my financial turnaround was embracing the powerful wealth creation concepts I share in this book. More than anything else, building true wealth begins with your mindset. You have to believe you are worthy of building wealth.

I wrote this book in a 31-day format to give you bite-sized doses of wealth empowerment inspiration so learning new financial concepts won't feel overwhelming. If building wealth has ever felt intimidating, this book will dismantle those obstacles as you read each daily insight. If you're ready to create wealth that lasts and enjoy more financial freedom and security than you ever thought possible... let's dig in!

Women Need to Talk About Money

The more we share our money journeys,
the more we can normalize wealth creation
and investment for people like us.

~Denise Duffield-Thomas,
Money Mentor and author of *Get Rich, Lucky Bitch*

In our society, it's taboo to talk about money, but it's okay to talk about your sex life. However, women need to talk about money to become aware of their options for building wealth.

Talking about money increases our financial literacy.

We need to continuously increase our knowledge about the various areas of personal finance and retirement planning.

We need easy access to and an understanding of options, resources, and strategies to help us secure a safe financial future.

We need to talk about money because, as women, we have been vastly underserved in the financial services industry. For the most part, the financial services industry is still male-dominated. Behind the closed doors of a financial planning meeting, a married woman will sit and listen to the conversation between her husband and the financial advisor. She never feels "in charge of her finances," even though she was present when vital financial decisions were made. It's even worse for single women. Many times, they feel too intimidated to even meet with an advisor. And when they do, they often leave the session feeling like the advisor was disrespectful or spoke over their head.

I'm not saying this is true one hundred percent of the time. More recently, the outdated ideology of men as chief financial decision-makers has shifted as women become more financially empowered.

Interestingly, women's long-term financial well-being has only recently become a concern for big financial institutions and insurance companies. This is likely because they know women stand to inherit a sizable portion of the $30 trillion in wealth transfer over the next decade. This realization means that more male advisors are finally becoming more sensitive to women's unique financial needs.

The bottom line is we women need to take responsibility and advocate for our financial security.

When we talk about money, it motivates us to take charge and get our finances in order.

Talking about money boosts our confidence and empowers us to make intelligent financial decisions. If you have ever experienced feelings of anxiety about money and your financial well-being, you're in the right place. This 31-day wealth empowerment journey is an opportunity to talk about money, learn about money, and get excited about your wealth creation plan.

Choose to Believe You're Worthy

What's keeping you from becoming rich? In most cases, it's simply a lack of belief. In order to become rich, you must believe that you can do it, and you must take the actions necessary to achieve your goals.
~Suze Orman, Personal Finance Expert

As I mentioned earlier, creating wealth begins with shifting your limiting beliefs. Your beliefs dictate your behavior, and your behavior will allow you to take action to reach your goals. If you don't do the necessary work to address your limiting beliefs first, you'll spin your wheels and wonder why you're not getting anywhere. Repeat the following affirmations to yourself daily to begin shifting your identity as a wealthy woman. You need to see yourself as a woman worthy of wealth before you can actually *have* wealth.

Affirmations

I am Worthy of Wealth

I deserve to step into my power and have wealth. I use my wealth for the greater good and appreciate it. I am worthy of abundance, prosperity, and riches. As my wealth grows, I can handle money and manage it well.

I do not allow my mind to focus on fear and scarcity. Instead, I choose to focus on wealth.

I attract wealth with grace and ease. I am a money magnet who draws wealth. I am committed to continually working on my wealth mindset, which allows me not just to bring money in but also to hold onto it.

Money is just one aspect of my wealth.

I also have an abundance of wealth in the form of love, joy, family, friendships, and health. Blessings flow into my life every day, and I'm grateful for them.

Wealth and prosperity come to me in many ways.

I let go of the self-limiting beliefs that block wealth. I release the negative thoughts that prevent abundance from being a part of my life. I invest time and energy into cultivating a healthy money mindset.

I am aware of how my actions and thoughts shape my wealth and financial success.

Starting today, I believe I deserve wealth. I know I deserve abundance in my life. I am grateful for the many blessings that flow into my life. I attract more wealth and abundance with each step I take.

My Coaching Tips

❖ New wealth affirmations may not initially feel 100% true. Don't let that discourage you; it's normal. Simply choose the ones you feel will support you the most right now and keep saying them out loud as you go through the process of imprinting new beliefs.

❖ If you feel doubt creep in or resistance to accepting a new, empowering money belief, simply ask yourself, "What if this could be true for me?" This will instantly refocus your brain on all that is possible for you to experience.

Days 1 Through 31

DAY 1

Why Wealth Empowerment
Is a Must for Women

You will never be powerful in life until
you are powerful with your own money.

~Suze Orman, Personal Finance Expert

Wealth empowerment gives you options you might not otherwise have. When you're wealthy, you can navigate any season of life with confidence and security because you'll get to enjoy advantages such as:

1. Financial Independence

Creating your own wealth enables you to assert your independence and gain control over your financial destiny. It allows you to make decisions based on your own goals and priorities rather than relying on others.

2. Emotional and Mental Well-Being

By taking charge of your finances, you can reduce the stress and anxiety often associated with financial uncertainty. Feeling in control of your financial future can improve your overall emotional and mental well-being.

3. Future Planning and Goal Achievement

Creating wealth helps you build a strong foundation, which provides you with a framework for future planning and achieving new goals. You can set clear financial goals, such as saving for retirement, buying a home, or funding your children's education. With a strong foundation, you can make informed decisions and take the necessary steps to turn your aspirations into reality.

4. Improved Quality of Life

As you build wealth, you create financial stability, which enhances your overall quality of life. It allows you to indulge in experiences and activities that bring you joy and fulfillment. Whether it's pursuing hobbies, travel, or investing in personal development, a solid financial foundation provides you with the resources to enjoy life to the fullest, which you deserve.

5. Setting a Positive Example

By creating your own wealth, you become a role model for your children and others who look up to you. You demonstrate the importance of financial responsibility, resilience, and the ability to overcome challenges.

Becoming financially empowered equips you with the tools and knowledge needed to create a secure, joy-filled future. It empowers you to make informed decisions (no more foolish money mistakes!) and achieve your goals.

DAY 2

How to Create a Wealth Mindset

We've already discussed mindset. Because it's so important, we'll discuss it throughout this book. As mentioned before, wealth creation starts with the mind. If you have an attitude of abundance, you'll be able to attract the financial success you deserve.

While there are many paths to wealth, once you discover the abundance mindset, you've set yourself up for *actually* achieving your dreams. But how do you create a wealth mindset in the first place?

The following techniques can help you develop a wealth mindset:

1. Visualize Your Goal

It's not enough to just say you want to be rich. You have to make the conscious decision to create a clear goal and visualize yourself in possession of it.

2. Be Specific

Break down your goal into manageable details and start thinking about the exact steps you need to take to achieve it.

3. Break Up the Plan

If the goal seems too big at first, break it down into smaller, more manageable steps. Focus on each task you need to complete, and then celebrate your wins once you achieve each step.

4. Take Action

It's easy to get caught up in the daydreaming and planning phases of your goals, but implementation is what it takes to get you there. Your dreams become realities with action.

5. Focus on Your Thoughts

Do you really believe that you can achieve wealth? Are negative thoughts holding you back? If necessary, remind yourself that wealth is possible and success is also a very real possibility for you. Pay attention to your thoughts because they can derail your efforts.

6. Choose to Believe You Deserve It

Believe that you are worthy of achieving wealth. If you don't think you deserve it, you may unconsciously set yourself up for failure. Do you truly want wealth? Then, be willing to follow through on your action plan while maintaining a positive attitude.

Believe in Yourself

Remember, wealth building starts with your mindset. Keep focused on your goals, and you'll build inner conviction and unstoppable momentum on your journey toward wealth empowerment.

DAY 3

5 Steps to Heal Your Relationship With Money

It's time to forgive ourselves for believing that we are 'bad with money' because it's not our fault. We need to heal our relationship with money so that we can stop underearning and become millionaires.

~Rachel Rodgers, Author of *We Should All Be Millionaires*

As women, we often juggle multiple roles. We may be parents, spouses, business owners, service providers, volunteers, caregivers, etc. While doing our best to keep up with these duties, it's not uncommon to deal with feelings of inadequacy around money. But if we want to create wealth, we must first heal our relationship with money.

Understanding the Root of Money Problems

The first step in healing our relationship with money is understanding why we associate negative feelings with it. Social conditioning, lack of financial education, or past experiences (especially childhood) can shape our views on money. But once you can recognize these influences, you can move forward.

Here are five steps to get you there.

Step 1: Embrace Financial Literacy

KNOWLEDGE IS POWER. Invest time in learning about personal finance, investments, retirement planning, and money management. You don't have to become an expert overnight. Just be eager to join the conversation. Start with the basics and gradually build your understanding. There are hundreds of articles about women, money, and building wealth on my site at https://pattifagan.com/category/women-money/.

Bookmark this page and create a ritual of reading one article each day with your morning coffee or tea. The five minutes it will take to read an article will be enough to increase your financial education gradually.

Step 2: Reframe Your Money Mindset

Replace negative beliefs with positive affirmations. Instead of saying, "I'm bad with money," tell yourself, "I am learning to manage money more effectively every day, and I'm enjoying it!" I know it sounds too simple to make a difference, but there is power in consistently using affirmations to reframe your money mindset.

Step 3: Practice Daily Gratitude

As a financial coach who has worked with women of all income levels, I have witnessed that those with a higher net worth demonstrate an attitude of gratitude toward money. This article talks about the power of gratitude combined with journaling: https://pattifagan.com/the-power-of-gratitude-journaling/

Step 4: Set Clear Financial Goals

Define what financial success would look like for you. Is it owning a home, building your dream business, or retiring early? Break these goals down into achievable steps to maintain focus and motivation. Create a vision board and add your goals to cultivate the inspiration you need to go after your dreams and goals. Here's a helpful article on what you should do before setting your money goals: https://pattifagan.com/do-this-first-to-reach-your-money-goals/

Step 5: Show Yourself Compassion

The most powerful thing you can do to heal your relationship with money is to show yourself compassion. Pat yourself on the back for doing the best you know how to do. Even if you've made money mistakes in the past, you deserve forgiveness. Women often don't realize how harsh they are with themselves around money. When coaching women over the years, I have found they tend to criticize themselves harshly. They create stories about being a bad person because they have debt and over-spend or feel clueless about money. Their inner critic keeps them stuck. Instead, we need to get to a place of forgiveness for our past money mistakes. When we can forgive ourselves for our past financial blunders, it empowers us. Self-compassion allows you to rewrite negative patterns and heal your relationship with money.

Take one baby step today. Which one of the above five steps to heal your relationship with money can you put into practice? Creating the wealth you deserve is completely within your reach— you just need to take the first step.

DAY 4

7 Financial Planning Rules to Live By

Money is like a game. And in any game, there are rules to follow if you want to win. No matter how the game goes, you have the best chances of winning when you live by the time-tested rules that govern it—the rules of financial planning. These rules will keep you on track despite market fluctuations, pandemics, inflation, and economic downturns.

Rule #1: You Must Have a Budget

If your expenses exceed your income, you'll always be in debt, and building wealth will be an impossible task. Create a budget and decide how much you'll allocate to needs, wants, savings, and paying off debt. Stick to this budget, monitor it daily, if not weekly, and try your best not to deviate from it.

Rule #2: Save at Least Ten Percent of Your Net Income

When getting started with a savings plan, the percentage is less important than creating the habit. Some people may be so deep in debt that even saving ten percent is difficult initially. If that's the case, aim for five percent or, at the very least, try to save ten dollars or even five dollars a month. It's the action that counts at first, not the amount. When you have even a small amount of money set aside, you'll shift your mindset just enough to go from a lack mentality to one of abundance. Creating wealth is nearly impossible when you have a lack mentality. As you get better at saving, trim your expenses wherever you can and allocate the extra money between your debt repayment and savings. Eventually, you'll want to save twenty percent of your income and thirty percent.

Rule #3: Prioritize Paying Off Debt

Being in debt can be a soul-sucking experience. Trust me, I know firsthand what that's like. The credit card companies are NOT your friends. They'll delightfully send you the credit cards upfront, but the moment you have a hardship, they become your worst nightmare. The late payment fees, the interest rates, the calls from the extremely rude debt collectors, and the never-ending bills in the mail will all pile overwhelming pressure on you that never lets up. It's a grueling and stressful experience I never want you to have to go through. The best way to avoid this is to pay your credit card bills in full and on time EVERY. SINGLE. MONTH. If you have more debt than you can pay off in a month, create a debt repayment plan and stick to it. It'll take time but know that if you're committed to getting debt-free, you'll come out of it slowly but surely. If you don't tackle this problem head-on, the credit card companies will harass you for a very long time, and you may even end up filing for bankruptcy. Thank God, I never had to, but I know many women who have. It's not a pleasant experience.

Rule #4: Don't Be Impulsive

When you have money to invest, do NOT risk it all. Avoid following hot stock market tips. Just because your smart friend or family member is high on an investment doesn't mean you should be, too. Do your due diligence. Educate yourself with a ton of research. Always proceed with caution. Diversify your portfolio and aim for gradual growth rather than fast cash, which usually means riskier investments.

Rule #5: Become a Saver, Not a Spender

Avoid overindulging in desires for material stuff like new cars, expensive clothes, shoes, and handbags, even houses you really can't afford. Trying to keep up with the "in" crowd is an almost surefire way to financial ruin, especially if your income doesn't support it. There's no point in buying what you don't need, with money you don't have, just to impress others. Spend wisely and avoid impulsive purchases. This is how you become a Saver instead of a Spender. This is how you create financial peace of mind. This is how you build wealth. Trust me, your future self will thank you.

Rule #6: Increase Your Income Each Year

Always seek to improve your knowledge, skills, and expertise so you can bring more value to your work. Almost every financial problem is solvable when you have enough income. When you're building wealth, earning more will accelerate your progress. So, do the best you can to boost your income each year. If for no other reason than to keep up with inflation.

Rule #7: Find Ways to Grow Your Money

You accomplish this by investing in assets such as stocks, your business, or real estate property, for instance. The key is to put your money to work for you. Be cautious, though. But also, don't be overly risk-averse, or you'll miss out on lucrative opportunities. As stated above, do your homework before investing and seek to improve your financial literacy before you make important financial moves. Armed with sufficient knowledge, you'll be able to make more informed decisions that serve you well in the future.

Which of these seven rules are you already honoring in your finances? Which one do you want to work on next?

DAY 5

Manifesting Wealth From Within

"Be thankful for what you have; you'll end up having more.
If you concentrate on what you don't have,
you will never, ever have enough."

~Oprah Winfrey

Manifesting wealth begins from within. And it starts with gratitude. You have to appreciate what you already have in your life–your family, friends, and job–instead of focusing on what you don't have that you want. Too many people waste energy thinking about what's missing in their lives. They believe their lives will only be better if they have more money or more stuff. They think about what's lacking instead of the abundance already flowing into their life. It might seem counter-intuitive, but wishing for more doesn't attract wealth into your life—gratitude for what you already have does.

Positive Thinking Brings Abundance

If you feel grateful for what you have, you'll be inspired to take the necessary actions to bring more of what you want into your life. At first, this may sound backward, but living contently with what you have doesn't mean you can't have more. It simply means that you appreciate all the good in your life, which ironically attracts more of the same.

Very often, we take our lives for granted and forget to give thanks for all that is good. If you're having a hard time seeing the good in your life, make a gratitude list and continue adding to it every day. For example:

- Be thankful when paying your bills because this means you have a place to live.

- Be thankful for your car because you don't have to walk everywhere.

- Be thankful for your family because you have their love and support.

- Be thankful for your job because it allows you to provide for your family.

If you can be happy with what you have now, you'll have a deeper appreciation for the better things coming your way.

First Steps Toward Wealth

When you don't have a lot of material possessions and monetary wealth, it ironically becomes easier for you to learn how to save money. Saving money is one of the keys to building wealth. But to do so, you have to learn how to delay gratification. Make sure you're making more money than you're spending. Ideally, you want to pay for everything you have. By going into debt, you're actually moving farther away from wealth.

Besides saving money, the real way to build wealth is to make more money. That may sound obvious, but too many people aren't making the money they can and should. Make a conscious decision to get unstuck from the ceiling on your income and set the intention to increase it every year. You have to set yourself apart and do something different. That may mean discovering creative ways to make more money. For many women today, starting a side hustle or an online business is the ticket to creating more wealth.

Define what wealth looks like for you, and if you're unhappy with the money you're making, start thinking about ways to increase your income so you create wealth that lasts.

DAY 6

Are You Comfortable with Success?

Do you believe you are worthy of success? Limiting beliefs prevent some women from imagining themselves as financially successful. For whatever reason (usually going back to childhood), we carry messages about our worthiness into adulthood.

When doing inner work around money, a pattern of deprivation often shows up. Perhaps emotional needs were not met by your primary caretakers, which creates a pattern of depriving yourself as an adult. When setting goals around money, an inner child part shows up as resistance because it's trapped in a pattern of deprivation.

Deprivation can show up in the form of a continual lack of finances. Consciously, you may be aware that the thought of success feels strangely out of your reach. Deprivation feels familiar.

Eliminating the fear of success can be as simple as replacing this pattern of deprivation and unworthiness with updated, powerful messages of self-love and self-acceptance. This is why I promote the practice of self-love. It has the power to heal your relationship with wealth and success.

Consider the following mindset shifts about success to become more comfortable with choosing success so you can build wealth.

The Fear of Success Can Manifest Itself in Different Ways

Procrastination, self-sabotage, and an inability to concentrate on important tasks (brain fog) are signs of resistance. Do you suddenly feel tired when performing a task that could take your success to the next level? These are signs that an inner part of you is derailing your efforts.

Question Your Limiting Beliefs

Make a list of your limiting beliefs regarding success. Get curious and question them.

❖ How do you know this belief is true?

❖ What if this belief was not true?

❖ Where did this belief come from?

❖ What empowering belief could I replace this limiting belief with?

❖ What is it costing me to hang on to this belief?

Acknowledge That Success May Feel Unsafe to You

It can seem safer to play small. The more successful you become, the more visible you become. You're more exposed to criticism and judgment. You have more responsibilities that you may be unable to keep up with. You'll have less free time. You may have to live with more pressure. These are all factors to acknowledge.

It may be helpful to remind yourself that you'll have access to more resources when you're successful. More resources can result in more safety. When you have plenty of money and influence, life becomes easier because you have more choices.

You Might Worry About Having to Become a Different Person

Yes, you'll become different because you've grown into a more evolved version of who you are today. However, you can still be the same person if you remain true to your authentic self.

Have a Vision of Success That Inspires You

Are you afraid that massive success will result in losing free time? Create a vision of success that allows you to work on your own schedule. Build time and location freedom into your vision. Success won't happen if your vision of success doesn't inspire you and pull you forward.

Get Clear on Your WHY

List all the benefits of success. Make a personal list that excites you. Remind yourself of all the advantages that success can bring: more money, peace of mind, comfort and security, more choices, contribution, and the ability to take care of your loved ones. What else comes to mind?

Don't underestimate how much your inner programming about success can sabotage your wealth. Be intentional about doing the inner money work. Create a vision of success to keep yourself motivated on the days it feels hard. Question your limiting beliefs. You deserve wealth and the success it will take to get there.

DAY 7

Overcoming the Fear of Success

The journey to success can sometimes be daunting. But the fears that come up don't have to keep you playing small. Success is found on the other side of fear, so let your fears be a compass to guide you to what you really want.

Following are 30 affirmations to help manage the fear of success, failure, visibility, vulnerability, and financial responsibility:

1. I trust in my capabilities and recognize the value I bring to the table.

2. Every step forward is a step towards success, no matter how small.

3. My vulnerability is my strength; it allows me to connect genuinely with others.

4. I am prepared and equipped to handle increasing financial responsibilities gracefully.

5. I am deserving of success and all the benefits that come with it.

6. My worth is not defined by the failures or setbacks I encounter.

7. I am constantly growing, learning, and evolving.

8. I am more than enough just as I am, and I do not need to prove my worth to anyone.

9. Every "no" I encounter brings me closer to a "yes."

10. I am not alone in my fears, and seeking support when needed is okay.

11. My voice matters, and my story is worth sharing.

12. I give myself permission to shine brightly and unapologetically.

13. I am capable of achieving my financial goals through perseverance and hard work.

14. I embrace the unknown and see possibilities, not threats.

15. Success is a journey, not a destination, and I am exactly where I need to be.

16. I will not let fear dictate my pace; I move forward courageously.

17. I am becoming a woman of resilience, strength, and empowerment.

18. My services are valuable and worth investing in.

19. I am brave enough to show up, even when it scares me.

20. I am resilient, bouncing back from setbacks with even greater wisdom and insight.

21. My success will be a beacon and an inspiration for others.

22. I trust in my vision and my ability to make it a reality.

23. I am a magnet for opportunities and success.

24. Being visible allows me to connect with those I am meant to connect with.

25. I am ready to handle the growth and success coming my way.

26. I am proud of what I've built and eager to share it with the world.

27. I am becoming a stronger and more confident version of myself every day.

28. I am open to receiving abundance in many forms.

29. I choose faith over fear, even in the face of uncertainty.

30. I trust in the timing of my life and know that everything is unfolding as it should.

Repeat these affirmations daily to help you overcome the fear of success and instill a mindset of self-assurance and resilience.

DAY 8

Cultivate These 7 Habits of the Wealthy

If you think about it, your life is largely the result of your habits. If your money habits aren't in alignment with building wealth, you'll never achieve your wealth goals. When it comes to achieving your goals, it's helpful to study those already doing what you want to do and then model what they do. To that end, the following are seven habits of the wealthy:

1. Focus on Assets

Wealthy people do not consider cars an asset. To someone who has wealth, an asset is something that creates income or additional value. Your vehicle does not meet this definition. Spend your money on tangible assets like stocks, bonds, businesses, precious metals, and similar items. Focus on buying assets instead of buying stuff.

2. Self-Improvement

Rather than being content with watching TV every night or going out for drinks with friends, wealthy people are more likely to read a book about business or self-development or spend their free time learning how they can bring value to the marketplace. If you want to be wealthy, regularly spend time becoming a better version of yourself.

3. Creating Value

The more value you create, the more you can expect to get in return for that value. Wealthy people create value and then charge for it.

4. Being Paid for Results, Not for Their Time

The average person spends their energy trading their time in exchange for compensation. The biggest challenge with the mindset of trading time for dollars is that time is limited. There are only so many hours a week, which caps your ability to earn beyond that.

5. Taking Calculated Risks

The average person does everything possible to avoid risk at all costs. However, a lot of money can be made when taking risks. Smart risk management is a common practice for wealthy persons. There's a huge difference between playing to win and playing not to lose. Those who play to win (wealthy people) create wealth.

6. Making Their Own Wealth

Ordinary people believe that wealth is something that happens to the lucky few. But the wealthy believe in taking charge and making things happen. They believe in making their own luck.

7. Never Giving Up

When trying something new, do you give up when it gets too hard? The wealthy person keeps going when challenges arise. They'll likely keep altering their approach until it works, but most importantly, they keep going. If you give up easily, you reduce your chances of building wealth.

Anyone can become wealthy with the proper habits in place. Start looking for ways to incorporate these habits into your life and watch how they impact your wealth over time.

DAY 9

7 Ways to Declutter Your Life to Make Room for Abundance

Your real life begins after putting your house in order.

~Marie Kondo

Have you ever noticed how wealth and abundance seem to flow more effortlessly for some people while others struggle endlessly to pay their bills? It might seem like wealthy people are born under a lucky star. But in fact, some principles govern wealth and abundance. One of those principles is living a life free of clutter. Money represents energy, and clutter is said to represent physically and emotionally stuck energy. How you handle your money—and your thoughts about it—can impact how abundance flows in your life. Decluttering enhances the flow of energy in any particular environment.

When applied to your finances, it can positively impact your mindset around money, which is important because, remember, creating wealth begins with your mindset. This simple concept may not apply to everyone because some of us are already pretty neat and organized when handling money. But believe it or not, some people treat their money with seemingly no respect whatsoever. Like a friend of mine who used to actually crinkle her dollar bills into a wad and throw it into her purse. Her money was a mess! (And so were her overall finances!)

Try the following strategies to allow more wealth and prosperity into your own life.

1. Declutter Your Wallet

Let's take a look at your wallet. What does the appearance of your wallet say about how you care for your money? Where do you put your receipts when you're out and about? Is everything neatly tucked in its place? Or is your wallet a catch-all for old receipts and other pieces of paper? And how do you treat your money? How do you store your dollar bills? Are they all organized and neatly arranged? Or are they a crumbled and crinkled mess? Finding a mess every time you go into your wallet creates a sub-conscious drain on your energy concerning money. Let's get your money in order with these quick tips:

- ❖ Get rid of your old, worn-out wallet and buy a pretty new one that makes you feel good about where you store your money.

- ❖ Clean out your wallet regularly so it doesn't become a cluttered mess.

- ❖ Keep your bills neatly arranged.

How you treat your money says a lot about how you treat your
finances in general.

Money is attracted to order, not chaos and clutter. So, if you want
your relationship with money to feel more harmonious, declutter
the energy by cleaning out your wallet.

2. Get Organized

Keeping everything you own in order makes everyday living easier
and less stressful. There's a place for everything, and everything is
in its place. This leaves room in your life for abundance.

3. Throw Out Old Stuff

If you don't use it anymore, get rid of it. Clear out clothing, books,
old files, household gadgets, and anything else you no longer need.
Things that are old, broken, or unable to be cleaned up properly
are just decluttering your mind and your space.

> *"But when we really delve into the reasons for why
> we can't let something go, there are only two:
> an attachment to the past or a fear for the future."*
>
> ~Marie Kondo

4. Give Away Some of Your Possessions

Whether you pass along magazines you've already looked at or
clothing you no longer wear, spread some of your wealth. When

you give to others, your heart opens up, and good things can more easily enter your life.

5. Find a Place for Possessions That Are Important to You

Provide each of your cherished items with a "home" within your home. When you take care of what you have, you're acknowledging and showing respect for the abundance already in your life.

6. Use What You Have

Take advantage of the items you've collected over the years. You obviously see them as having value, so why not put them to good use? You'll feel more positive about life and will get in touch with the abundance you already have when you make use of your possessions.

7. Stop Making Mindless Purchases

This one might seem obvious, but spending money mindlessly can become a bad habit that will eventually get you into trouble. I know because I used to do this myself. Wasting money on mindless purchases erodes your wealth. Make a vow to avoid compulsively buying the next new thing. If you always want the latest item on the market, look inside yourself and see why that is. Practice self-reflection journaling to notice how you feel when you want to buy another new item. Where is this desire coming from? What makes you feel compelled to spend money? Are you looking for a dopamine hit?

Then, figure out another way to get it that won't derail your wealth goals. Try things like exercise, getting sunlight, listening to music (I'm listening to a chill jazz playlist on Spotify as I write this!), gratitude, reaching your goals, eating protein, and supplements such as tyrosine, iron, and vitamin B6. Utilizing natural ways to increase dopamine levels in your brain will keep you from seeking feelings of pleasure and reward through buying things.

As you begin to truly cherish your possessions and take care of your money, home, and overall environment, you'll find yourself feeling more expansive than ever. Your mind will be in alignment with creative thoughts, which allows the flow of abundance.

DAY 10

Is Your Attachment Style Hindering Your Money Relationship?

Our financial well-being is deeply connected to our emotional health. Our relationships, both with people and money, are guided by deeply ingrained patterns. These patterns, or attachment styles, are formed in our early childhood and influence how we connect with ourselves, others, and the world around us, including our financial behaviors. If you've ever wondered why you do what you do around money, perhaps your attachment style is to blame.

Attachment Style Theory was founded by psychoanalyst John Bowlby in the 1950s and expanded by Mary Ainsworth. Attachment styles are not permanent labels but insights into better understanding ourselves. Recognizing and understanding these attachment styles as they pertain to money can shed light on the drivers of our financial behaviors.

Let's look at the four types of attachment styles and how they may manifest in your relationship with money.

1. Secure Attachment

If you find yourself comfortable with money, and you are able to both save and spend within reason, you may have a secure attachment style. This reflects the ability to show up consistently in your relationship with money and handle it responsibly. Those with a secure attachment find money is neither a source of anxiety nor a manipulation tool. Embracing this attachment can lead to financial stability and harmony.

2. Anxious Attachment

People with an anxious attachment style tend to feel overly anxious about money and resist dealing with it because the thought of doing so triggers feelings of overwhelm. Those with anxious attachment feel unworthy of love or wealth due to low self-esteem, and they tend to put other people's needs before their own, meaning they give money to others before their own needs are met. Increasing self-worth by implementing self-love practices and self-care, which can include financial self-care, will help shift this attachment style over time.

3. Avoidant Attachment

Those with avoidant attachment fear intimacy, so they avoid getting too close to others, including money. If you often ignore financial matters, avoid budgets, or feel detached from monetary goals, you may have an avoidant attachment. To transform avoidant attachment, begin nurturing a more engaged relationship with your finances, where you create new habits of simply showing up with your money, which can look like setting money goals, tracking expenses, and checking your online bank accounts each day, for instance.

4. Disorganized Attachment

This attachment style can be confusing and may reflect contradictory behaviors and feelings toward money. If you find yourself acting impulsively with finances, swinging between extremes of anxiety and avoidance, you may have a disorganized attachment. Often stemming from childhood trauma or inconsistent (unpredictable or unsafe) caregiving experiences, this pattern can lead to a tumultuous relationship with money, marked by unpredictability and stress.

Divorce, especially when traumatic or complex, may exacerbate disorganized attachment. It's essential to approach this attachment style with compassion. Working with a therapist can provide a safe space for you to explore difficult emotions around relationships with people and money. Understand that a disorganized attachment doesn't mean you're doomed to financial instability. However, recognizing this pattern is a powerful first step in seeking healing and transformation.

The good news is your attachment style is not your destiny; it's a framework that helps you recognize your unhealthy patterns around money. With self-awareness and compassion, you can heal and adapt to a healthier way of relating to money.

For more information on Attachment Style Theory, this article on PsychCentral.com will explain it in more detail. It includes an attachment-style quiz (scroll to the end of the article for the quiz). https://psychcentral.com/health/4-attachment-styles-in-relationships

DAY 11

How to Create Secure Attachment in Your Money Relationship

Yesterday, we looked at how attachment styles impact our relationship with money. I shared how these patterns are formed in our early childhood and influence how we connect with ourselves and the world around us, including our finances.

To help you shift your behavior around money, I'm sharing some suggested methods for changing from an insecure attachment style (insecure, anxious, or disorganized) to a more balanced, secure attachment.

1. Identify Your Attachment Style

Understanding whether your insecurity stems from an anxious, avoidant, or disorganized attachment to money will allow you to approach healing in a targeted way.

2. Seek Professional Guidance

A financial therapist or counselor can provide personalized support, helping you navigate complex emotions and create a tailored plan for moving toward security.

3. Create a Financial Plan

Establishing a clear, manageable budget that aligns with your goals can reduce anxiety and provide a sense of control, which can reduce anxiety and overwhelm.

4. Build a Support System

Surround yourself with understanding friends, family, or support groups who can offer encouragement and wisdom as you make changes.

5. Embrace Financial Education

Knowledge is empowering, especially financial knowledge. Take the time to learn about personal finance, retirement planning, investments, and savings strategies that align with your goals.

6. Practice Mindfulness

Mindfulness exercises can help you recognize triggers and respond with intention rather than reacting impulsively. Mindfulness practices can include journal writing, engaging in a creative activity, and gratitude.

7. Set Achievable Goals

Break down your financial objectives into small, manageable steps. Celebrate each little achievement, no matter how small, recognizing that progress is a journey, not an overnight transformation.

8. Emphasize Self-Compassion

Acknowledge that your attachment style is not your fault. It was how you adapted to your primary caregivers' behavior beginning in infancy. Changing from insecure to secure attachment takes time and effort. Be gentle with yourself.

9. Explore Emotional Connections

Dive deeper into how your emotions are linked to money. Journaling or reflective exercises can help you understand underlying fears or desires.

10. Implement Boundaries

If needed, set clear boundaries with others regarding financial matters to avoid undue stress or pressure. Most importantly, always take care of your financial needs first before giving money to others. One topic that comes up frequently in coaching sessions is the idea of loaning money to your adult children. You may want to read my article, *Should Women Loan Money to Their Children:* https://pattifagan.com/should-women-loan-money-to-their-children/

11. Consider Debt Counseling

If debt is a part of your financial anxiety, seeking specialized support to manage and reduce it can alleviate a significant burden.

12. Heal From Past Traumas

For disorganized attachment especially, it may be essential to work with a mental health professional to address underlying traumas that impact your relationship with yourself, other people, and money.

13. Embrace a Growth Mindset

Believe in your ability to change and grow. Cultivate a positive outlook, knowing that you're on a path to a more balanced relationship with money.

By integrating these methods into your life, you are not merely changing a financial strategy; you are embracing a holistic transformation that honors your emotional well-being and personal growth.

By identifying and understanding your attachment style, you're not only taking a crucial step toward healing but also empowering yourself to reshape your financial future.

DAY 12

30 Affirmations for a Healthy (Secure) Relationship with Money

For the last two days, we've been exploring attachment styles and how they impact your relationship with money. This list of 30 empowering positive affirmations is designed to foster a healthy, secure attachment with self, other people, and money. They also focus on increasing self-love, reducing fear of abandonment, and eliminating financial avoidance behaviors.

Declare these affirmations daily out loud or write them out by hand. Let them serve as reminders of your intrinsic worth, inner strength, and resilience.

1. I am worthy of love and financial security.

2. I trust myself to make wise financial decisions.

3. I embrace a healthy relationship with money and see it as a positive force in my life.

4. I am confident in my ability to provide for myself and my loved ones.

5. I love and accept myself unconditionally.

6. I release the fear of abandonment and trust in the stability of my relationships, especially my relationship with money.

7. I am in control of my financial future and actively engage with my financial well-being.

8. I am deserving of success, love, and prosperity.

9. I attract positive relationships that support my growth and well-being.

10. I am resilient and can handle life's challenges with grace and wisdom.

11. My self-love grows daily, allowing me to share love with others freely.

12. I am secure in my relationships and know that I am loved.

13. I face my financial responsibilities with courage and clarity.

14. I am constantly growing and learning in my relationship with money.

15. I forgive myself for past mistakes and embrace the opportunity to learn and grow.

16. I am not defined by my fears or insecurities; I am empowered by my strengths and values.

17. My relationships are balanced and filled with understanding and compassion.

18. I am open to receiving abundance in all areas of my life.

19. I am connected with divine wisdom and trust this wisdom to make decisions that align with my true self.

20. I release the need for validation from others and find it within myself and my relationship with my Creator.

21. I prioritize my emotional well-being and take actions that support my mental and financial health.

22. I am free from the fear of lack and embrace a mindset of abundance.

23. I am at peace with my past and excited for my future.

24. I create financial goals that reflect my values and work actively to achieve them.

25. I am grateful for the abundance in my life and trust that God blesses my financial growth.

26. I am committed to building healthy, supportive relationships with others.

27. I recognize that I am enough, just as I am, and do not need to fear abandonment.

28. I approach money matters with curiosity and enthusiasm, not avoidance.

29. I believe in my ability to create a life filled with love, security, and prosperity.

30. I am loving, lovable, and loved, and I allow financial success to flow into my life.

By declaring these affirmations with intention and belief, you're cultivating a profound shift in your identity to encompass self-love, healthy relationships, and financial empowerment.

DAY 13

3 Simple Steps to Calculate Your Net Worth

Make it a policy to know your net worth to the penny.

~T. Harv Eker

Knowing your net worth is the first step towards becoming financially healthy. You cannot guesstimate this process or just have a 'feel' for it.

You'll actually need to do the numbers here. So often, women avoid finding out their net worth because they fear knowing where they stand. Or they think it might be too big of a task to handle. In reality, it's quite easy and straightforward. Today, you'll discover how to calculate your net worth in three simple steps.

But first, you must know the difference between assets and liabilities. In its simplest terms, an asset is something that has exchange value, generates income for you, or has the potential to generate income. Liabilities are financial obligations—everything you owe, such as car payments, credit card debt, etc.

Here's a quick list of assets and liabilities:

Assets

- Life insurance
- Cash on hand
- House and/or rental property
- Land
- Gold
- Individual Retirement Accounts (IRAs)
- Savings bonds
- Stocks and/or mutual funds
- Possessions you can sell
- Vehicles (car, boat, RVs, etc.)

Liabilities

- Loans (student loans, lines of credit, home equity loans)
- Credit card balances
- Mortgages
- Student loans
- Taxes
- Child support
- Alimony
- Any bills, etc. that you OWE

Calculating Your net worth

Now that you understand what assets and liabilities are, it's time to begin.

Step #1

Grab a piece of paper and draw a line down the center, dividing it into two columns. In the left column, write down the cash value of ALL your assets.

Don't be too concerned about whether it's paid in full or not. Just write down the cash value. For example, if you could sell your car for $17K, this asset has a value of $17K. It doesn't matter if you still owe $9K on your auto loan—just write 17K in the left column.

Do this for ALL your assets. How much could you sell your home for? What's the cash value of your life insurance policy? *Note: If you have stocks, bonds, etc., look at the current value of the assets, NOT the value at maturity.*

Step #2

Repeat the process in the right column, but list all of your current liabilities.

Remember the earlier example of the car?

In the liabilities column, you would write "Car 9K" ... because you still owe $9K on it. The same applies to all other liabilities.

If you still owe $70K on your home, this, too, will go in the right column, even if you wrote "Home $400K" in the asset column earlier.

Step #3

This is where we determine our position. All your assets are listed on the left, and each has a number attached... All your liabilities are on the right, and those have numbers, too.

In Step #3, we'll total up all the numbers in the left column. Write the sum total at the bottom of the assets column.

Do the same thing for the numbers in the liabilities column to get the total of your liabilities.

Now, subtract your liabilities from your assets. **This is your net worth.**

For example, if your assets total $520K and your liabilities total $310K...

$520K - $310K = $210K

Your net worth is $210K.

However, many people may discover that their liabilities exceed their assets.

For example, if their assets are at $150K, but their liabilities are $320K...

$150K minus $320K equals -$170K.

That means they have a net worth of -170K.

Now, you can make a plan.

If your liabilities include 'bad debt' such as credit card bills, student loans, etc., you'll definitely want to create a financial plan to pay off the debt as soon as possible.

The goal is to reach a positive net worth and keep increasing it as much as you can. This will enable you to reach your wealth goals and eventually retire comfortably. But it all starts with knowing where you stand now. Repeat this exercise annually.

DAY 14

5 Powerful Investing Resources for Women

As I mentioned earlier, women face unique financial challenges that men do not. For instance, women still earn less than men, which means they retire with fewer assets. This is why women need to take advantage of resources that can help them create financial wellness by making their money work hard for them.

According to the National Institute on Retirement Security report, women at retirement age are 80 percent more likely than men to be in poverty.[3]

The same report states that 401(k)-type retirement accounts have balances thirty-four percent less than men's, and women are three percent less likely to be eligible for their employers' retirement plans than men are. Aside from unequal pay, factors like longer lifespans and leaving the workforce to care for children or aging

---

[3] https://www.nirsonline.org/reports/shortchanged-in-retirement-continuing-challenges-to-womens-financial-future/

parents put the balances of women's retirement funds at a disadvantage, also according to the NIRS.[4]

But please don't let all that get you down because it is absolutely possible for women to overcome these challenges. Women-focused organizations offer tailored investing products and advice. With investment-planning algorithms that take into account the gender wage gap or messaging that reaches women on a personal level, they're here to help.

Listed below are five resources that can help women catch up their retirement accounts.

1. Ellevest

Helps women create personalized investment strategies. (https://www.ellevest.com/)

2. She Spends

Makes personal finance more approachable. (https://shespends.org/)

3. Savvy Ladies

Offers financial webinars for the busy woman. (https://www.savvyladies.org/)

---

[4] https://laborcenter.berkeley.edu/pdf/2016/NIRS-Women-In-Retirement.pdf

4. Women's Institute For Financial Education (WIFE)

Builds strong financial literacy foundations.
(https://www.wife.org/)

5. Women's Institute For A Secure Retirement (WISER)

Offers nationwide research and workshops.
(https://wiserwomen.org/)

Ladies, these websites are loaded with content and resources to help you be better with your money and become a better investor so you can grow your wealth.

Please, please, please take some time on your day off and go through these websites and take advantage of the resources they offer. This is how you build your financial literacy, which enables you to build wealth.

DAY 15

7 Financial Goals to Achieve Before Retirement

Financial planning for a successful retirement can seem overwhelming. However, if you break it down into achievable milestones, it'll be easier to stay focused and accomplish your goals. One of the biggest concerns women come to me with is that they're getting a late start. But I tell them it's never too late, especially if they are committed and have a plan. But the opposite is true as well. The earlier you start planning for retirement, the better. Not only will you have more time to save, but you'll be able to recover from any mistakes or losses you might make along the way. (Money mistakes are a part of life!)

Following are seven financial goals to achieve before retirement.

1. Save 6x to 10x Your Annual Income

Experts say that if you earn $60,000 per year, you should save anywhere from $360,000 to $600,000 in a retirement fund. This may seem like a lot, but with time and a solid plan, it's possible to save this amount.

2. Pay Off Debt

The faster you eliminate debt, the easier it will be to save. You can then redirect the money for your debt payments to your wealth creation plan. You'll be amazed at how much faster your wealth can grow when your income is not burdened by debt.

3. Start a Roth IRA

A Roth IRA will allow you to save your money and let it grow tax-free. But the best thing is you'll enjoy tax-free withdrawals in retirement because money put into a Roth IRA has already been taxed. Keep in mind that you must meet certain income requirements to be able to invest in a Roth IRA. After your income exceeds a certain amount, you'll be disqualified from Roth contributions. You can find the IRS guidelines here:

https://www.irs.gov/retirement-plans/traditional-and-roth-iras

4. Estate Planning

Creating an estate plan is like writing a love letter to your loved ones after you pass. Hire a professional to help you with estate planning and deciding how your assets will be distributed to your beneficiaries. Even if you don't think you're wealthy enough, an estate plan will make things go smoothly when it comes to deciding what to do with your home, bank accounts, and other assets once you pass on.

5. Take Advantage of a 401(k) Match

This is one of the best ways to max out your retirement account. If your employer offers a 401(k) match, you should contribute the maximum amount allowed to your annual 401(k) plan. Your employer will then match a percentage of your contribution, and you'll have more savings in your 401(k).

6. Invest Wisely

Once your emergency savings is fully funded, you'll want to consider where to invest your money so it can grow and keep up with inflation. However, you should first assess your risk tolerance and ensure you know what you're investing in.

7. Save on Fees

When investing, your goal should be to reduce any fees as much as possible. Avoid investments that have loads and investments where the brokers get a commission. Be cautious and exercise due diligence here.

DAY 16

Investing in Funds 101

Funds are one of the most common types of investments used by people to grow their money. When a group of people pool their money together to invest, that is called a fund, and there are several types of funds. For instance, mutual funds, stock funds, bond funds, exchange-traded funds (ETFs), and money market funds. Most funds operate similarly–where the money is collected and managed by fund managers. Beginner investors typically opt for mutual funds because they can leave the investment management to the money managers. There's also the added benefit of diversification for safety.

For example, a mutual fund may invest the money in a dozen or more securities in different markets. In this way, not only is your investment diversified, but you'll be able to own shares in different companies. When you invest in a fund, a fund manager buys shares in different companies on your behalf. One benefit of having a large number of people pooling their money is that the fund manager can invest in more expensive shares that yield better returns.

Following is an explanation of the most common types of investment funds.[5]

Mutual Funds

As noted above, mutual funds combine cash from a large group of investors and invest in stocks, bonds, and other securities. Shares of mutual funds are bought and sold at the end of each trading day.

Money Market Funds

Money market funds are fixed-income mutual funds that invest in low-risk, short-term debt and can be easily turned into cash. Money market funds typically offer low returns.

Index Funds

Index funds are a type of mutual fund whose investments track a particular market index, such as the S&P 500. Index funds are a passive way to invest in the stock market.

Exchange-Traded Funds (EFT)

ETFs are similar to mutual and index funds, except they can be traded like stocks throughout the day over a stock market exchange.

---

[5] https://www.nerdwallet.com/article/investing/fund

Real Estate Investment Trusts (REIT)

REITs invest in real estate and income-producing properties like apartment buildings, hotels, or malls. They are often compared to mutual funds because they typically hold a selection of real estate investments.

Hedge Funds

Hedge funds pool funds from pre-qualified investors, typically high-net-worth individuals and organizations. Hedge funds typically employ riskier trading strategies and charge high performance-based fees.

DAY 17

Stop Trading Time for Dollars

Many of us were taught to do well in school, get a good job, work hard, and we'll eventually make a lot of money. This may be true, but there is a challenge to working for someone else—time. There are only so many hours in a week. You cannot buy or create more time.

Many medical doctors struggle with this. The average physician earns a decent salary, but not many earn $1 million per year by seeing patients. That's because physicians swap their time for money. They only get paid while they're seeing patients. They can't see more than one at a time and can't see patients while they are asleep. Their income is limited by the number of hours they can show up to work. This is also true for consultants, dentists, and lawyers. To build wealth that will give you true financial freedom, you'll want to find ways to earn without personally being present to do the work necessary. What you want is time freedom.

Here are a few ideas.

1. Get Paid More Than Once for the Same Work

Artists, authors, content creators, and musicians get paid over and over again for the same work. An author can write a book and then sell one million copies over the next ten years. I know many fiction writers who publish three to four books a year and earn well over six figures from book royalties. These authors get paid over and over for the work they did once. What could be better than getting paid multiple times for the same work?

Insurance agents also get paid more than once for their work in the form of commissions on renewals from the policies they sell, which is one reason people go into this field. I know a property and casualty agent who owns an insurance agency with one of the big-name carriers. She's owned her agency for almost thirty years and now earns multiple six figures a year just from renewal income. She spends a few hours a week at the office at most. A friend of mine started her career in insurance later in life (in her early 50s), and now, after four years in the business, she earns over $200k a year selling Medicare insurance. She carries minimum overhead because she works from home. Since she earns renewal income, she doesn't trade time for dollars.

2. Do Something That Allows You to Receive Recurring Payments

Airbnb rentals or renting out other real estate provides an ongoing income stream. Sarah Weaver, a real estate investing guru and author of *30-Day Stay: A Real Estate Investor's Guide to Mastering the Medium-Term Rental* travels the world living off of her income from mid-term property rentals, which she rents out to traveling nurses and executives.

3. Invest in the Stock Market

The great thing about stocks, bonds, mutual funds, and similar investments is the ability to make money passively. You're essentially making money while you sleep. You could also loan money to others and make money on the interest you charge. I know one investor who got tired of the uncertainty of the market and started making short-term loans to real estate investors. He makes an average of 20% to 25% on his money with safe investments because the loans are secured by the property.

4. Outsource / Arbitrage

Many people set up businesses and outsource all the work. This works especially well for online businesses. For example, some people sell website-building services and hire someone else at a reduced rate to do all the work. Another example is some authors pay ghostwriters to write their books. Then, they sell those books as their own. The listed author paid someone else to write the book. If you can successfully buy something for $X and sell it for $X+Y, you can potentially make money with little work.

5. Create Passive Income Through Affiliate Marketing

Affiliate marketing involves earning a commission for promoting another company's product or service, usually via an email newsletter, social media posts, or on your website. Michelle Rohr is an excellent example of someone who has capitalized on the power of affiliate marketing, earning $1MM in sales in just a few years. A self-taught graphic artist, Michelle combined her passion for personal development and printable life planners and founded her company Secret Owl Society. She eventually added gorgeous digital planners to her product line and now earns an additional passive income stream by creating her own digital courses and enlisting others to sell them for an affiliate commission. Affiliate marketing has become quite popular because it's a great way to generate passive income without having to do the work yourself.

Homework: To get started, choose a passive income strategy that feels doable for you. Learn everything you can about that strategy. Then implement, tweak, repeat, and prosper!

DAY 18

How to NOT Run Out
of Money in Retirement

Retirees don't live on assets; they live on income!

—Tom Hegna, Author of *Don't Worry, Retire Happy:
Seven Steps to Retirement Security*

For the average American, lifetime income (income that will last as long as you're alive) will come from one of three sources:

1. Social Security

2. A pension from their place of employment

3. A guaranteed lifetime income annuity (provided by an insurance company)

The media has given a bad rap to annuities, but contrary to what you may have heard about them (from financial celebrities who run ads on television, for instance), they're not all bad. In fact, the new ones on the market (like equity-indexed annuities) can be a powerful component of your retirement portfolio.

David Swenson, Chief Investment Officer at Yale University and the expert interviewed for the article, *How To Not Run Out Of Money In Retirement,* believes it would be a wise move to include an advanced life deferred annuity in your retirement portfolio.[6]

A guaranteed lifetime income annuity is a contract between you and the provider (usually a life insurance company), which guarantees you a certain amount of income (received monthly, quarterly, or annually—you choose) in exchange for a certain amount of money (called a premium). You pay the insurance company a premium in either a lump sum (single premium) or over a certain period (flexible premium).

The biggest benefit of lifetime income annuities—aside from providing safety to your principal, so you can't lose money when the market drops—is that you can elect to receive income for life. For as long as you're alive, you'll receive a check from the insurance company even after your balance goes to zero. If you die before receiving all the money you put in, the remaining balance goes to your beneficiaries. With an annuity contract, the insurance company is insuring the risk of you outliving your money. This is HUGE for women who want to safeguard their retirement income. **Using the power of an annuity, you can create a lifetime income stream that acts like a pension.**

---

[6] https://www.npr.org/2016/04/26/475759586/how-to-not-run-out-of-money-in-retirement

Several additional benefits can enhance a basic annuity contract, such as:

- ❖ Joint life payout, which continues payment to the second spouse when the first spouse dies

- ❖ Riders for long-term care expenses such as nursing home

- ❖ Inflation protection rider

The more benefits you add to the contract, the more you reduce your overall payout. It's all a matter of priorities and what you're trying to accomplish in your portfolio.

One of the biggest complaints about annuities is their complexity, which causes a lot of confusion for consumers (and for many advisors, too!). But there are plenty of highly trained advisors who know how these financial instruments work—or at least they should know how they work.

A second complaint is their high fees. Not all annuities have high fees. Variable annuities are notorious for high fees, averaging four percent nationwide. I don't recommend variable annuities, and neither do many advisors. Most of the other annuities in the marketplace have low fees, in the one percent range. So, don't believe everything you hear, especially when it's in a television ad.

A third complaint about annuities involves the commissions paid to the advisor. Yes, advisors earn a commission when you purchase an annuity. Don't you think they should be compensated for the training and education it took for them to be able to serve you? The commissions do not come out of your pocket. They are paid out of the insurance company's general fund. We don't have a problem paying real estate agents a commission when they sell your house. In California, we pay a six percent commission on the sale of a home. That's about what an advisor earns when they open an annuity account for you, which is paid by the insurance company. Why would you have a problem with that?

A fourth complaint about annuities is they can be confusing. How do you know which to choose and which features should you include? Your financial advisor can walk you through your options. Contact your advisor to find out how much guaranteed lifetime income you could receive based on your unique scenario. There is no cost, and you don't have to commit to anything to get an illustration showing you your options and how these lifetime income annuities work. Your future self will thank me. You're welcome!

Here are a few resources to help you learn more about how annuities work:

1. *Don't Worry, Retire Happy: Seven Steps to Retirement Security,* by Tom Hegna (pages 74-86 explain different types of annuities and how they work in layman's terms).

2. *Income Allocation: Enhance Your Retirement Security,* a book written by one of my former mentors, David Gaylor.

3. **Fidelity** provides helpful information about annuities at https://www.fidelity.com/annuities/overview

4. **AnnuityWatchUSA.com** has a plethora of retirement planning resources, articles, and videos, including a video series on the different types of annuities at https://www.annuitywatchusa.com/watch-your-videos/.

Here's yet another opportunity to educate yourself on all the different options available to help you secure your financial future.

The above is an excerpt from my book, "How Every Woman Can Retire Without Worry: 10 Simple Steps to Secure Your Financial Future," which is available on Amazon.

DAY 19

Explode Your Limiting Money Beliefs

Here's a great mind-expanding exercise that one motivational speaker teaches in his prosperity thinking workshops: Get out a piece of paper and write down your current annual income.

Now imagine making that figure in one month rather than one year. For example, if you wrote $50,000 as what you made last year, then imagine making $50,000 in one month. How does that feel? Really allow yourself to imagine making $50,000 a month. Ask yourself, *"What if this could be true for me?"* How much are you willing to envision making $50,000 a month? Imagine how that might feel. What are you willing to believe? You have to believe that right at this very moment, this is a possibility for you.

Applying This to Your Business

If you're a woman in business, you have to believe that at this very moment, there are clients–your perfectly ideal clients–praying for a solution to their problems. And that solution is YOU. Your job is to share your talents, skills, and expertise with them.

It starts with being willing to explode your limiting money beliefs, which will expand your ability to receive the income you deserve while sharing your brilliance with the world. Upleveling your mindset to believe that it's possible. Make a decision that it's possible for you to have more money flowing into your life.

Uplevel your money mindset by asking yourself new questions:

❖ What do I need to believe to have my yearly income become my monthly income?

❖ What decisions would someone who earns that income make in their business?

❖ What habits would someone who makes that income have?

❖ What do I need to let go of to have that new income?

❖ What do I need to do more of to have that income?

When you want to take your income to the next level, work on your mindset every day. It's not a one-time thing. This is a daily process of evolving your beliefs to support your new goals. Create a new identity to step into, an identity that aligns with what God created you to be—a wealth-empowered woman.

DAY 20

How a Spending Plan Empowers You

If we command our wealth, we shall be rich and free.
If our wealth commands us, we are poor indeed.

~Edmund Burke

Wouldn't it be great to have enough money to live your life to its fullest while still putting away plenty for a rainy day? You *can* turn this goal into your reality if you're willing to create a spending plan and stick to it. A thoughtful spending plan enables you to make financial decisions that support your values, dreams, goals, and peace of mind. With a spending plan, you see exactly where your money goes, which helps you spend less on items that don't fit your life's priorities or core values. As a result, you have more money to spend on things that matter to you.

Knowing where you spend your money builds a strong foundation for wealth empowerment.

When you work with a spending plan, you create a habit of healthy spending and saving to support you in pursuing your dreams. A simple spending plan ensures funds are available for spontaneous pleasures and planned (and unplanned!) expenditures.

The first step in creating your spending plan is gathering the necessary items. These include your bank statements, bills, and information about how much cash you have available. It's also helpful to know how much you're spending on necessities like food and gasoline.

The spending plan you create can be as simple as writing it down in a notebook or a spreadsheet on your computer. The important thing is that it helps you track what you spend and keep your financial life organized.

Using a Spending Plan to Meet Goals

When you know where you're spending money, you're more likely to achieve your financial goals. Also, *remember that it's okay to adjust your plan.* You don't have to do everything perfectly from the beginning. Know that it probably won't be perfect. The effort to get your finances under control will lead to peace of mind and security in the future if you stay organized and adjust your plan as you go.

Your spending plan is the first step to the financial freedom and peace of mind you deserve. Knowing where you spend your money empowers you. It gives you options a fantastic sense of financial security.

DAY 21

8 Common Investing Mistakes to Avoid

Investors should remember that excitement and expenses are their enemies.

~Warren Buffett

Investing in stocks, bonds, funds, and other financial instruments is an excellent way to grow your money over the long term. However, keep in mind there is a degree of risk involved. I always tell my clients to have three to six months' worth of income in an emergency fund before they start investing.

If you want to be extra cautious, having another ten thousand dollars in a certificate of deposit (CD) will give you a cushion to handle any unexpected financial scenarios.

Once you have the funds to invest, avoid making the eight most common mistakes.

1. Not Understanding What You're Buying

Before buying shares in a business, you must understand what the business is all about. While you don't need to understand the intricacies of running the company, you should have an idea of what they do. People think Warren Buffet is just a super smart guy who just seems to get lucky with his stock market picks. What they don't know is that Warren spends most of his time reading reports on the companies before investing in them. You must be well-informed before investing. Don't invest based on 'hot tips' you get from people who don't know what they're talking about.

2. Mixing Savings and Investments

Money in savings and money in investments serve two entirely different purposes. Your savings are meant for emergencies, so keep it in the bank (or in a fireproof safe at home) where it's liquid and you can access it fast. While inflation may slowly chip away at its value, cash in the bank is far safer than cash in investments. Do not risk your savings to invest. Keep them separate.

3. Lacking Patience

Creating wealth from investing takes time. Consider investing as a long-term plan. Looking at investing as a 'get rich quick' scheme will have you making impulsive choices and get you into trouble. You shouldn't invest the money you'll need in the next few years. Slow and steady wins the race.

4. Putting All Your Eggs in One Basket

Avoid putting all your money in only one stock. Companies can collapse. It's best to diversify your investment portfolio by investing in mutual funds or ETFs. Other options to consider if you're nervous about investing are high-yield savings accounts, short-term certificates of deposit, or money market accounts. I like the balanced approach suggested in this CNN article for new investors: https://www.cnn.com/cnn-underscored/money/investing-for-beginners

5. Not Monitoring Your Investments

This is a common mistake many people make. They invest in stocks and after a while, they get busy or bored and forget to monitor their investments. Lynnette Khalfani-Cox, author of *Bounce Back: The Ultimate Guide to Financial Resilience*, says, "You should monitor the assets you own to make sure nothing gets out of balance and to avoid duplicating investments."

Markets fluctuate, and you may need to rebalance your portfolio. You may need to sell losing stocks and purchase winning ones. Investing is not set it and forget it. It's more hands-on than that.

6. Having Unrealistic Expectations

Don't expect to become a millionaire overnight. While you should invest your money, you'll also want to find other ways to increase your income. Diversification is the name of the game. The more income streams you have, the faster you'll build wealth.

7. Trying to Time the Market

Unless you have a very good understanding of the markets, it's very difficult to time the market. As I said before, investing is a long-term plan. It's best to keep your wits about you and take the long, gradual, and sensible approach.

8. Not Thinking Long Term

Again, investing yields the best rewards over the long term. Don't trade too much and too frequently. Choose stocks in companies that show promise and watch their performance over the long run. As they do better, the share price will increase, and your investment will appreciate in value.

These eight mistakes can ultimately sabotage your chances of success when investing. So, use them as a guide to keep yourself in check.

DAY 22

Savvy Real Estate Investing Tips

Real estate investing, even on a very small scale,
remains a tried and true means of building
an individual's cash flow and wealth.

~Robert T. Kiyosaki

Real estate has historically been proven to be a reliable investment for creating wealth. According to a Lending Tree survey, 45% of Americans believe investing in real estate is the top choice to grow wealth.[7]

Many of the wealthiest people (think Barbara Corcoran and Robert Kiyosaki) have made their money from real estate. Ben Lovro, a real estate investing guru, says that 90% of millionaires attribute their wealth in part to real estate investments.[8]

---

[7] https://www.lendingtree.com/debt-consolidation/wealth-survey/

[8] https://www.linkedin.com/pulse/what-real-estate-creates-90-millionaires-ben-lovro/

What makes real estate a solid choice for growing wealth?

Among others, some of the benefits include:

- Being a true source of passive income.

- Real estate tends to hold its value over time. Although there will be slumps and market declines. When the market picks up, so does the price of property.

- There's a finite amount of land (limited supply).

- However, there is no shortage of financing. If you can show the banks that you're creditworthy, they'll extend loans to you.

- Real estate property is a tangible investment.

- Property values rise with inflation.

Real Estate Investing Tips

Make Sure You Have No Personal Debt

Do not invest in real estate if you still have student loans, credit card debt, etc. Eliminate all bad debt first so that you don't overextend yourself.

Don't Take On Too Much Risk

Relying solely on occupants to pay your mortgage is not always wise. For instance, the recent pandemic affected many real estate investors who bought short-term rental properties to offer as Airbnb accommodations. But suddenly, there were no occupants.

Create a Business Plan and Figure Out How You'll Make Your Monthly Payments

Established investors are able to pay for a property in full – though most still take loans because the interest on loans pales in comparison to what they can make by investing their money elsewhere.

If you're new to real estate investing, the best thing you can do is to get a mentor who is actively investing in real estate. One such woman is Tressa Todd. I love her story so much! She is a woman killing it in the world of real estate investing. Her story is so inspiring. I shared it in my book, "How Every Woman Can Retire Without Worry," and I want to share it here, too:

> Real estate investing changed Tressa Todd's life. At fifty years old, she quit her corporate job of twenty-five years and joined her three sons in real estate investing. An industry she knew nothing about. You see, she thought she was getting ready to retire from her corporate job in the medical field. Instead, she got a rude awakening when her son, Kelton, went through her finances and discovered that she didn't have nearly what she needed to retire. She thought because she had a 401(k) and some savings, she would be set for life. Boy, was she wrong.

Even though she was intimidated by the idea of going to work in real estate, she discovered that meeting with people and negotiating was actually fun and exciting.

In Tressa's words:

"In four months, I made more money than what I had saved in my 401k after twenty-five years in my medical career. I was in shock and asked myself, "Why didn't I start this sooner?" Are you wondering how I did it? By finally getting the courage to start investing in real estate. At fifty years old, I took the leap of faith and quit my twenty-five-year career in the medical field to start investing in real estate. And I did it without risking my own money or credit. In fact, in the first deal I made, I didn't even have to do anything to the house. I didn't paint…I didn't have to repair anything. I didn't even mop the floor. I simply found the deal, got it under contract, and then assigned that contract to an end buyer. Eight days later, I received a $20,000 check from my first real estate deal. That's it! It's called Wholesaling. And that is only one of the strategies that I teach. The best part of all is that you don't need a real estate license or any previous real estate knowledge to get started… I sure didn't! If you are willing to learn and apply the strategies I teach, any woman can be successful in real estate investing!"

Tressa's mission is to help women become financially confident and create multi-generational wealth by encouraging them to be brave, knowing that doing hard things brings great blessings. You can learn more about Tressa's masterclass at WithoutFearOfHerFuture.com.

Tressa wrote a book that teaches the basics of how she invests in real estate, *Without Fear of Her Future: A Women's Guide To Real Estate Investing.*

Another source for learning how to invest in real estate is Bigger Pockets. They offer training programs to support real estate investors at all levels.

Check them out at https://www.biggerpockets.com/.

Investing in real estate is a fantastic way to grow your money. But do your homework first—I can't stress that enough.

DAY 23

Become a Magnet for Wealth

So much of creating wealth is about believing you are capable of having wealth and then stepping into the identity of a wealthy woman. I created this list of wealth mindset shifts to help you continue to imprint new beliefs about wealth and money.

Affirmations for Becoming a Magnet for Wealth

Starting today, I see myself as a magnet for wealth and luxury.

I attract beautiful items that represent wealth on my terms into my life and incorporate these luxuries into my home and lifestyle.

My home is an opulent and comfortable haven that inspires me.

I remove the blocks that prevent wealth from being part of my life. I attract prosperity and beauty with each thought.

I am able to rise above money struggles by shifting my thoughts about wealth.

I have the wisdom, courage, and creativity to make my wealth dreams a reality. I have the ability to use my skills to create more wealth.

I love the incredible freedom, amazing possibilities, and powerful choices that having money makes so richly available to me.

I am a money magnet that attracts new opportunities in my business and personal life.

I am open to the positive influences of wealth. I acknowledge the role of money in making my life more comfortable and less stressful.

I love feeling wealthy.

I have the power to change my lifestyle and improve my family's financial circumstances. I have the ability to make my life secure and free from worry about money issues.

Today, I notice wealth in every aspect of my world. I attract it with each thought and action.

DAY 24

6 Tips to Get Your Retirement Planning on Track

According to experts, retirement planning is a bigger concern for women than for men. I've been telling my readers this for years. Generally, there are three main causes for women's financial vulnerability in retirement.

1. Women outlive men.

2. Women make less than men over the course of their working years.

3. Women retire with less in savings (and less to live on) than men.

How do we, as women, find ourselves in this predicament?

In my blog article, *Women & Retirement – Helping Women to Not Outlive Their Money,* I share a CBS News Money Watch interview with Rebecca Jarvis. Visit the article on my website at https://pattifagan.com/women-retirement-helping-women-to-not-outlive-their-money/

According to the CBS News Money Watch interview with Rebecca Jarvis, CBS News & Business Economics Correspondent, there are two societal influences:

> Financial illiteracy is higher among women. Wharton research shows that women are less literate about finances than men, which means they don't invest as wisely over the course of their lifetimes.

> As I mentioned earlier, women are socialized not to talk about money. Money is considered a taboo topic. As such, it's not a topic they are accustomed to having with others. We can talk about sex, yes. But not money.

Here are six tips for women to get their retirement planning on track.

Tip #1 – Get Educated and Make a Plan

There are plenty of resources online to help you increase your financial literacy (go back to *Day 14: Powerful Investing Resources for Women*). Make it a daily habit to consume financial content. One way to do that is to subscribe to my weekly newsletter at PattiFagan.com.

Tip #2 – Pay Off Debt

Having high debt payments is the last thing you want in retirement. This is a time when you should be reducing your expenditures and living expenses. Focus on paying off your debt with the highest interest rate first. Next, pay off the debt with the next highest interest rate, and so forth. In this way, you're getting rid of the most expensive debt first. Also, call each creditor and ask if they would be willing to reduce the interest you're paying. Explain that you're trying to get debt-free. It doesn't hurt to ask, right?

Tip #3 – Start Saving Today!

Don't wait. Don't make excuses. Start with 10% to 15% of your income. Have it automatically deducted from your paycheck. Don't underestimate the power of compounding interest. The sooner you get started, the better, and it's never too late.

Tip #4 – Take Advantage of Your Company Retirement Plan

Especially if they offer a match. That's free money for you. Plus, your money grows tax-deferred, which means you don't pay taxes on the contributions now. You'll pay taxes on the withdrawals (contributions and growth) when you take them.

Tip #5 – Just Do It!

Think about it. You will never regret cultivating the habit of saving money. Only good things will come of it.

Tip #6 – Get Smart About Social Security

Determining how to take your Social Security benefits is a complex decision with a myriad of possible scenarios. Making the right decision can mean a difference of up to $100,000 or more in Social Security income over the course of your retirement. Although trying to decipher your options can be daunting, it's definitely worth the time and effort. You can learn more by taking advantage of the information and resources provided at the Social Security website: http://ssa.gov/retire/estimator.html.

However, you should be aware that the Social Security Administration counselors are not financial planners and are not allowed to give advice.

It would behoove you to do a search in your area for a financial advisor who specializes in Social Security planning before making any final decisions.

Do your homework, sister! Your future self will thank you!

DAY 25

Do You Want to Retire Early?

*Don't simply retire from something;
have something to retire to.*

~Harry Emerson

Retiring early often conjures up mental images of sitting by the beach holding hands with your spouse as you watch the waves rolling on the shore. Or maybe you see yourself sitting on the front porch knitting... or rocking in your favorite rocking chair, reading a good cozy mystery. To enjoy a carefree retirement, you'll want to plan effectively and early. Far too many women underestimate how much money they'll need for retirement. Remember Tressa Todd, the real estate investor from Day 22? She thought that since she had contributed to her 401(k) for twenty years, she'd be set for life. The age at which pre-retirees choose to retire continues to go up as people realize they don't have enough money to retire any earlier.

Consider the following questions if you want to retire early.

Are Your Debts Paid Off?

The best thing anyone can do for their finances is eliminate debt as soon as possible. Debt here refers to personal loans, credit card balances, auto loans, and student loans. If you have student loan debt, aim to pay it off as soon as you can. The same applies for your mortgage. You'll be amazed at how much easier it is to put away for retirement when you don't have debt eating away at your earnings. Strive to pay off all debts as soon as possible.

Do You Have Enough Saved in Your Emergency Fund?

You should have a minimum of 3-6 months of your income saved up in case of an emergency. Twelve months of living expenses would be better. Your car may break down, or your roof may need to be replaced. Having savings will help to cover these unforeseen expenses.

Have You Made Plans for Assisted Living?

Since women live longer than men (which means our money needs to last longer), putting long-term care coverage in place is a crucial element of a sound retirement plan. Medicare does not cover long-term care expenses. I always tell my clients, "No retirement plan is complete without long-term care." Long-term care insurance provides options in your golden years and helps you maintain a life of dignity that you may not be able to afford otherwise. There are various types of LTC policies to help cover long-term expenses. Contact your local health insurance agent or financial advisor and they can walk you through your options. It doesn't cost you anything to get quotes, which will illustrate exactly what the premiums will cost and what the policy covers.

Have You Considered Downsizing?

One way to put more money toward your retirement is to down-size your home. If it's just you and your spouse, you may choose to sell your home and live in a smaller house or a condo. Another option to consider is retiring to a location where the cost of living is significantly lower. Portugal comes to mind. Many people I know have moved there and for good reasons: it's a beautiful country, fairly inexpensive, the people are friendly, and it boasts a rich culture and history. Apparently, it has a large ex-patriot community.

Do You Have Investments?

If you've invested in stocks that pay dividends or you're a savvy investor growing her money over time, you'll know how to make your money work for you. Investing knowledge will serve you well into your senior years because you'll know how to enjoy a good return on your investments.

DAY 26

Reap the Benefits of a Down Market

Be fearful when others are greedy
and greedy when others are fearful.

~Warren Buffett

When the market dips, most investors panic. But a bear market is when you can find the best investing opportunities. When the market declines, even great stocks can take a hit. The savvy, cool-headed investor knows this is when stocks are on sale.

Consider the following ideas to benefit from a down market.

1. Be Happy

The best investors get excited when the market is underperforming. Now is the time to find great deals. The best opportunities exist when fear grips everyone else.

2. The Time to Buy is When the Market is Down

But you can't just buy anything. It's still important to make smart investment decisions. Do your due diligence and be prepared.

3. Dollar Cost Average into the Market Because You Can't Predict Market Lows

Invest a specific amount each month. That way, you'll purchase more shares when the market is at its lowest.

4. Sell Off Your Mistakes

Even the best investors make bad investments. You can take the loss on your taxes. If you want to repurchase the same stock, you'll need to wait at least thirty days if you want the tax break. Put the proceeds from the sale toward more promising investments. Avoid holding on to stocks you feel don't have potential for growth.

5. Invest in an Index Fund

It's a pretty safe bet that the entire market will eventually recover. Every down market has turned itself around. Keep in mind that most index funds typically beat conventional mutual funds.

6. Stay Calm

It's not easy to keep a cool head when everyone else is panicking. But a panicked mind makes poor decisions. Panic in the marketplace can be a good thing. Let others make foolish decisions. You'll be ready to take advantage of those bad choices.

7. Rebalance Your Portfolio

A struggling market is a great time to rebalance your portfolio. Make the necessary moves to get back to equilibrium. You may take a few losses, but those losses can save you money on your taxes and put you in a stronger position for greater profits down the road.

When everyone else is worried, take advantage of sale prices. Keep a cool head, and you'll reap the benefits.

DAY 27

How to Stay Motivated on the Journey to Growing Wealth

Today, I'm going to share something about the drive that fuels us to build habits that lead to wealth. Now, I know the journey to financial freedom isn't always smooth – trust me, I've been there. But what if I told you that the secret sauce to creating wealth is already within you?

Understanding Your Why

Creating wealth begins with connecting with your WHY. Why do you want to be wealthy? For me, it wasn't just about having money. It was about security, freedom, and the ability to give myself choices.

The Power of Daily Habits

Doing the little things consistently creates big changes. Did you know that you're building a wealth habit just by setting aside a small amount of your income regularly? It's like planting a seed and nurturing it daily. Watching it grow can be incredibly empowering. I remember the first time I saved enough to invest.

I felt like I was taking control of my future, and let me tell you, that feeling is priceless.

Embrace the Learning Curve

Learning about finances can feel overwhelming. It's sort of like drinking from a fire hose. But here's the thing—nobody starts as an expert. Take it one step at a time. Read a book. Follow financial blogs. Subscribe to financial newsletters like the one at HerMoney.com. Knowledge is power, especially when it comes to your money.

Celebrate Small Wins

Don't overlook the small victories. Paid off a credit card? That's amazing! Saved your first $1000? Girl, that's fabulous! These milestones are proof of your dedication and progress. Reward yourself with little treats for each financial goal you achieve. Acknowledging your progress makes a difference. It makes the journey enjoyable and keeps you motivated.

Reflect on Your Path to Wealth

Honor your financial journey by taking time to reflect on it. I like to keep a separate notebook dedicated to my money work. Think about your wealth journey, your dreams, and how far you've come. Remember, wealth isn't a destination. It's a lifestyle. And the most beautiful part? It starts with the power you have within you to keep yourself motivated.

DAY 28

ETFs vs Mutual Funds 101

There are many similarities and differences between mutual funds and exchange-traded funds (ETFs). While the differences aren't dramatic, they can be important. Following is a high-level explanation to give you an idea.

A mutual fund is a pooled collection of assets that invests in stocks, bonds, and other securities. An exchange-traded fund (ETF) is a type of pooled investment security that can be bought and sold much like an individual stock. An ETF can be structured to track anything from the price of an individual commodity to a large and diverse collection of securities. ETFs can even be designed to track specific investment strategies.

The main difference between an ETF and a mutual fund is that though a mutual fund is also a pooled investment, it trades only once daily after market close.

Both funds can track indexes, but ETFs tend to be more cost-effective and liquid since they trade on exchanges like shares of stock. Mutual funds can offer active management and greater regulatory oversight at a higher cost.

Essentially, both permit an investor to own a wide variety of stocks and securities without requiring a large investment. So, which one is a better investment, mutual fund or ETF?

I'll let my wealth mentor, Linda P. Jones, chime in.

"Exchange Traded Funds (ETFs) invest in indexes like the S&P 500. Because there is no portfolio manager managing the fund, it merely mirrors the S&P 500. It is known as a passive managed fund because the stocks do not change. ETFs have gained popularity because many portfolio managers have not outperformed the S&P 500, so why pay them an additional fee when you are not earning more? Conventional wisdom says put your money in indexes that are lower cost and mirror the stock market's performance." *

For an excellent breakdown of the details and a comparison of the differences between a mutual fund and an ETF, visit the Charles Schwab website: https://www.schwab.com/etfs/mutual-funds-vs-etfs

*Taken from *You're Already a Wealth Heiress! Now Think and Act Like One*, page 44

DAY 29

Negotiating Tips for Women's Empowerment

Believe in your worth and negotiate your salary.
You are just as deserving as anyone else.

~Sheryl Sandberg, author and former COO of Facebook

Recently, I attended a training hosted by my dear friend and financial therapist, Barbara Huson. The topic was Negotiation Tips for Women, and it was taught by Kathleen Kingsbury, a wealth psychology expert and the author of *Creating Wealth from the Inside Out*. Today, I'm sharing tips from the pages of notes I took during her presentation.

These tips aim to help you cultivate your negotiation mindset so you can negotiate from a place of empowerment, not fear. With that in mind, let's discuss some practical tips and strategies for negotiating effectively as a woman, whether in the workplace, marketplace, or as a consumer.

1. Own Your Value

The first step to successful negotiation is to know your worth. Research the industry standards for the position you are negotiating and the current market value. Analyze your strengths, achievements, and contributions to the organization to build a strong foundation for your negotiation. Prepare a strong case for why you are the right person. Knowing your value makes it easier to make a compelling argument to support your request.

If you're a solo entrepreneur, coach, consultant, or speaker, knowing and conveying your worth is key to getting the fee you deserve for your services. It's highly recommended that you work on your mindset before entering any sales conversation with prospects. Rehearsing or role-playing what you'll say is an excellent strategy for building confidence.

2. Increase Your Confidence

Confidence is crucial when negotiating. Build your confidence by preparing in advance, practicing your negotiating skills, and identifying areas of strength. Having a strong sense of self-assurance makes it easier to maintain composure and come across as persuasive and convincing. Working with a business or money coach can help in this area.

3. Polish Your Communication Skills

Speak confidently and clearly. Maintain a steady tone and keep your body language relaxed and friendly. Making eye contact builds rapport. Be confident in presenting yourself as a worthy candidate, and don't be afraid to ask questions or express concerns. Practice negotiating with someone supportive to gain more confidence. Stay calm even if you feel uncomfortable. Give yourself permission to feel nervous.

4. Practice Active Listening

Active listening is a critical skill in negotiation. It will help you consider the other party and what's in it for them. When listening to the other person, you gain insights into their priorities, needs, and wants. You can tailor your approach to address their concerns while also advocating for your own needs. Active listening also builds trust and rapport, which can help create a more positive and productive negotiating environment. When you engage in active listening, you can create a collaborative conversation because you know what the other party wants from the arrangement.

5. Be Willing to Walk Away

Finally, be willing to walk away from the negotiation if necessary. This may seem counterintuitive, but if the other party is unwilling to meet your needs, it might be better to accept that the negotiation is unsuccessful. You always have a choice, and sometimes, walking away may be the better option.

All professional women should master the skill of negotiation because it will always be needed when endeavoring to build wealth. When you know your worth, increase your confidence, polish your communication skills, practice active listening, and are willing to walk away, you can negotiate from a place of empowerment.

Remember, the key to successful negotiation is preparation and practice, but mostly confidence in yourself.

DAY 30

Money Dates Are the New Sexy

If you're feeling a little overwhelmed after everything we covered in this book, that's completely normal, and I want you to know you're not alone in feeling this way. Financial topics can be utterly mind-boggling. But before we get ready to sign off, I want to share an important strategy to implement what you've learned, and it's a fun idea, too. Let me introduce you to the power of weekly money dates.

We have been taught that we shouldn't worry our 'pretty little heads' about money and that managing money is a man's job. When I was a retirement planner, more often than not, women, especially single women, relied on their fathers or brothers to step in and make decisions for them. They were afraid to make money decisions on their own because they believed a man needed to have the final say in their financial affairs. Ladies, this is a disempowering mindset that perpetuates the feeling of helplessness. This explains why many intelligent, intuitive, creative women struggle with managing and saving money.

The Power of Weekly Money Dates

Like any relationship, we need to invest time in our relationship with money. This is where weekly money dates can help. You'd be surprised at how empowering it is to hold weekly money dates. By repeating an action every week, you create new neural pathways in your brain, which takes the mystery out of dealing with finances because it becomes familiar.

If having a money date every week seems too much, try every two weeks. Even monthly money dates would be better than ignoring your finances altogether.

Financially empowered women take charge
with the power of weekly money dates.

All you need is ten to twenty minutes and a list of money tasks you want to take action on. However, if you want to make your money dates feel super supportive and empowering, add a cozy cup of tea (or a glass of wine, if you prefer!) and a nice soothing music playlist. The point is to do what you can to soothe your nervous system before and during your money date. This will shift you from any feelings of anxiety around money and bring your prefrontal cortex and executive functioning part of your brain online. Then, you can be fully present and think clearly about your money tasks and goals.

Your To-Do Items

* ❖ Schedule your weekly money dates on your calendar.

* ❖ Download *The Financial Organizer for Busy Women*. It's filled with worksheets, trackers, goal setting pages, monthly pages, and journal prompts to empower you on your financial journey.

Visit the link below to download it for free.

https://pattifagan.com/financially-savvy-women

DAY 31

Commit to Your Wealth Goals

Procrastination is the enemy of success, and the guilt of not doing something always steals your energy.

– Barbara Corcoran, American Business Woman, Investor, and Shark on *Shark Tank*

Now that we've come to the end of *31 Days of Wealth Empowerment*, you have a decision to make. Will you put this book back on the bookshelf and go about your business, never giving your wealth goals another thought? Or will you draw a line in the sand and commit to your wealth goals starting today so you can afford to live the life you've always wanted? Barbara Corcoran reminds us: *"Just go for it. You don't want to end up with regret."* Here are a few more affirmations to repeat daily to help you step into the identity of a go-getter wealth creator.

Affirmations for Committing to Your Wealth Goals

I am ready to commit to my wealth goals.

The time has come for me to commit myself to creating more wealth and bettering my life.

Consistent action creates more and more money for me and the people I care about.

I am doing the things that need to be done. I am thinking the thoughts that need to be thought. I am reaching out to the people whose help I need. I am directing all of my available resources to reaching my wealth goals.

I am feeling more motivated than ever to take my wealth and my life to the next level. Because I take excellent care of myself and only eat healthy foods, I am so full of energy I can barely contain myself.

I am committed to taking massive action. I am committed to my success.

My goals and aspirations for wealth are guiding my decisions. Before I make a decision, I consider how it will affect my progress toward my goals.

I know that my habits are the foundation of my success or failure. I am creating the habits necessary to ensure my success. I am dropping any habits that stand in my way. I am committing myself to a daily routine of positive, effective habits that support my wealth goals.

Today, I am fully committing myself to achieving all of my wealth goals and aspirations, no matter how out of reach they seem right now. I am taking action to the best of my ability, and I'm learning as I go.

Wealth-Building Journal Prompts

❖ What are the biggest obstacles to achieving my wealth goals?

❖ What can I do to overcome those obstacles?

❖ What is one baby step I can take in the next 24 hours?

❖ What resources do I need to gather first?

CONCLUSION

Now That You're a Wealth Empowered Woman

By embracing the tips and strategies in this book, you have empowered yourself to take charge of your finances, grow your wealth, and create a fulfilling life as an empowered woman. Keep in mind that wealth creation is an ongoing process, so surround yourself with a supportive network of like-minded women to keep yourself motivated.

Anything is possible if you really desire to create wealth. You have the power to shape your future and live a life of abundance and independence. Embrace your wealth journey with boldness, and may you thrive in all aspects of your life.

Thank you for joining me on this 31-day wealth empowerment journey.

I want to live in a world where every woman leans into her economic power to create wealth and success on her terms, which means financial security that is in her control, not someone else's.

Download Your Special Gift!

Remember to download *The Financial Organizer for Busy Women.* It's filled with worksheets, trackers, goal-setting pages, monthly pages, and journal prompts to empower you on your financial journey.

You can claim your gift for FREE at

PattiFagan.com/Financially-Savvy-Women

Here's to your financial empowerment!

Patti Fagan

About the Author

Patti Fagan is a Ramsey Solutions Master Financial Coach, Christian Life Coach, former retirement planner, insurance agent, and a thought leader on women, money, and retirement. She is a past member of the National Association of Insurance & Financial Advisors (NAIFA). She ran her own insurance and financial services agency for nine years, assisting women with creating a secure retirement. Audiences of professional women from various backgrounds have raved about Patti's seminars on topics such as:

- Understanding Your Cal-STRS (California State Teachers Retirement System)

- Growing Your Circle of Wealth

- Tax-Free Retirement

- The Unique Financial Challenges Women Face in Retirement

- Women, Money & Power

Patti mentored other financial professionals and was one of a select group of advisors in the country who are certified to provide retirement planning in public school districts.

As a writer, coach, and blogger, Patti is passionate about empowering women. She wants every woman to be financially secure, both now and in their retirement years. Her mission is to help them heal their relationship with money and own their economic power so they can enjoy financial peace of mind. Ultimately, Patti believes every woman has the capacity and intelligence to rule her own financial affairs.

To learn more about Patti's work, visit her website at PattiFagan.com.

Other Books by Patti Fagan

How Every Woman Can Retire Without Worry:
10 Simple Steps to Secure Your Financial Future

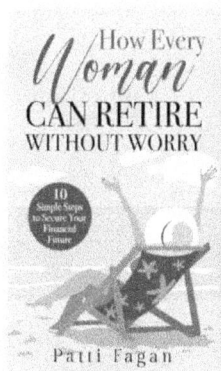

Are you ready to unlock the secrets to retiring with income for life, financial freedom, and peace of mind? If you're concerned about having enough money to support yourself when you can no longer work, this book will be your new best friend and blueprint for financial success.

Get started on your journey to financial empowerment today!

Get Your Copy on Amazon

https://www.amazon.com/Every-Woman-Retire-Without-Worry-ebook/dp/B0C9SPPF18

40 Days of Prayer for My Finances:
Powerful Prayers for Financial Breakthrough

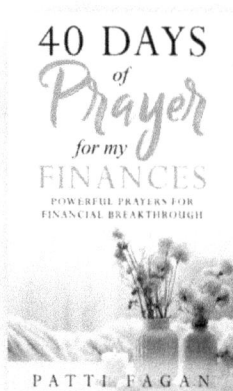

The relentless worry and stress about money can be overwhelming. I've been there, and I'm here to tell you there's a way out. Introducing *40 Days of Prayer for My Finances*, a powerful and transformative book of prayers designed specifically for Christians facing financial stress. This book is your key to breaking free from the chains of financial lack and discovering God's promises of prosperity and provision in your life.

Begin your 40-day journey to a financial breakthrough today!

Get Your Copy on Amazon

https://www.amazon.com/Days-Prayer-Finances-Financial-Breakthrough-ebook/dp/B0CPWC2RYH

Financially Savvy Women:
Mastering Your Money When Starting Over

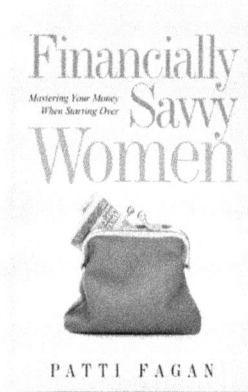

This book is your road map of financial empowerment. It's not just about budgets, retirement, and insurance; it's about reclaiming your independence and creating the life you deserve.

Are you ready to master your money starting today?

Get Your Copy on Amazon

https://www.amazon.com/Financially-Savvy-Women-Mastering-Starting-ebook/dp/B0CTL3CD5X

Healing Miracle Secrets

Did you know that God's will for you is healing and that He still performs healing miracles today?

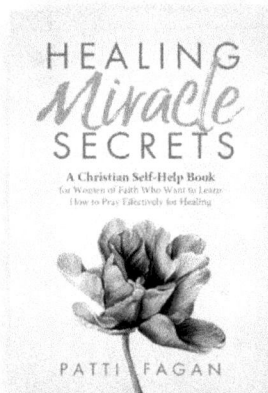

Healing Miracle Secrets will equip you to fight the good fight of faith, take back your health, and claim the life of divine health God has for you. Are you ready to learn how to pray effectively for your healing?

Get Your Copy on Amazon

https://www.amazon.com/Healing-Miracle-Secrets-Christian-Effectively-ebook/dp/B0BGT758W1

One More Thing

Was this book helpful to you?

Before you go, I want to thank you for purchasing my book. I sure do appreciate you! I hope reading this has inspired you to take a stand for your financial security.

You can support women's financial empowerment by leaving me a positive review on Amazon. Would you please take a moment to leave a review for this book? (Reviews are crucial for the success of authors on Amazon.)

Your feedback will help me continue writing valuable books that will empower women financially. If you enjoyed my book, please let me know. I would truly appreciate it.

Patti Fagan